This book belongs to

_____

Periwinkle's Chair

By Judith Zeilenga

Illustrated by Cheryl Cook

ISBN 978-1-64468-998-1 (Paperback)
ISBN 978-1-64468-999-8 (Digital)

Copyright © 1996 by The National Library of Poetry

Copyright © 2020 Judith Zeilenga
All rights reserved
First Edition

All rights reserved. No part of this publication may be reproduced, distributed, or transmitted in any form or by any means, including photocopying, recording, or other electronic or mechanical methods without the prior written permission of the publisher. For permission requests, solicit the publisher via the address below.

Covenant Books, Inc.
11661 Hwy 707
Murrells Inlet, SC 29576
www.covenantbooks.com

For Kate, Margaret, Brett,
Dahlia and Wyatt and all the other children and grandchildren who have lost a loved one to a terminal illness. The periwinkle ribbon you see throughout the book is the official ribbon of "Esophageal Cancer Awareness"

Can you find the periwinkle ribbon on each page?

In memory of Grandpa Neil in Heaven

*A special thank you to my editor
Kyle Lesniewicz*

There is a funny thing about some names.
My name is Periwinkle.
You might ask why I have such a funny name.
You see, periwinkle is a color and a flower.
My family named me Periwinkle after the flower.
Me and my mommy love flowers.
My grandpa always loved flowers too.
He kept a lovely garden, full of periwinkle.

My grandpa was a tall and strong man who worked hard every day to make a wonderful life for all of us. There was nothing he could not do to make things right. He was a kind and generous person who brought out the best in everyone.

One day, he went for a checkup with my grandma because he was not feeling quite himself.

He had to go for a test at the hospital. The doctor came in afterwards and said he was sorry, but he had some frightening news. They discovered that my grandpa was suffering from a terrible illness.

"Let's not get ahead of ourselves", he said. "I plan to fight this and win."

And so, he put up a good fight. He went through his treatments with tremendous courage. Until his final days, he had great hope he could fix it. The doctors would do everything they could to fix it too.

My grandpa could fix anything. Why not this?

He tinkered in his garage, in his house, and *especially* in his garden, fixing everything that needed attention. The illness he was facing he would not be able to fix.

But what he *could* fix was something very special for me before I was even born. So, he did.

This is the story of Periwinkle's chair.

My grandpa was often going to doctors' appointments and treatments. He could no longer work at his job, so he spent his days driving here, there, and everywhere and working on many projects to keep his mind occupied. He did not complain even when he was feeling tired. He still did all the things he loved to do and traveled about to wherever he desired.

On one of his regular routes, out of the corner of his eye, he noticed a pile of broken pieces of wood in the grass at the roadside. He drove by that spot many times after that, always pausing to get a better look as he passed by.

Finally, he excitedly told my grandma about his find and said, "We must go pick it up and bring those pieces home. I think it is a long-forgotten child's rocking chair. I will fix it up for our grandbaby who is coming soon."

And he gathered up that pile of broken pieces and brought it home. He laid it all out in front of him and wondered how he could ever put it back together again.

The chair seat was rotten and cracked and would have to be replaced. He found a piece of scrap wood in which he drilled holes. He shaped it and sanded it to make it smooth. It fit just right!

Then he delicately connected all the pieces together, bringing the chair back to life. He was careful to make it really safe. He was delighted with how it turned out.

After the chair was finished and the glue was dry, he said, "Now we must paint it!"

He put that soft brush to the surface of the chair. And instead of it being an old, scratchy, stained brown chair it became a bright and cheery, fresh and softer one. But not soft enough! It would need a cushion!

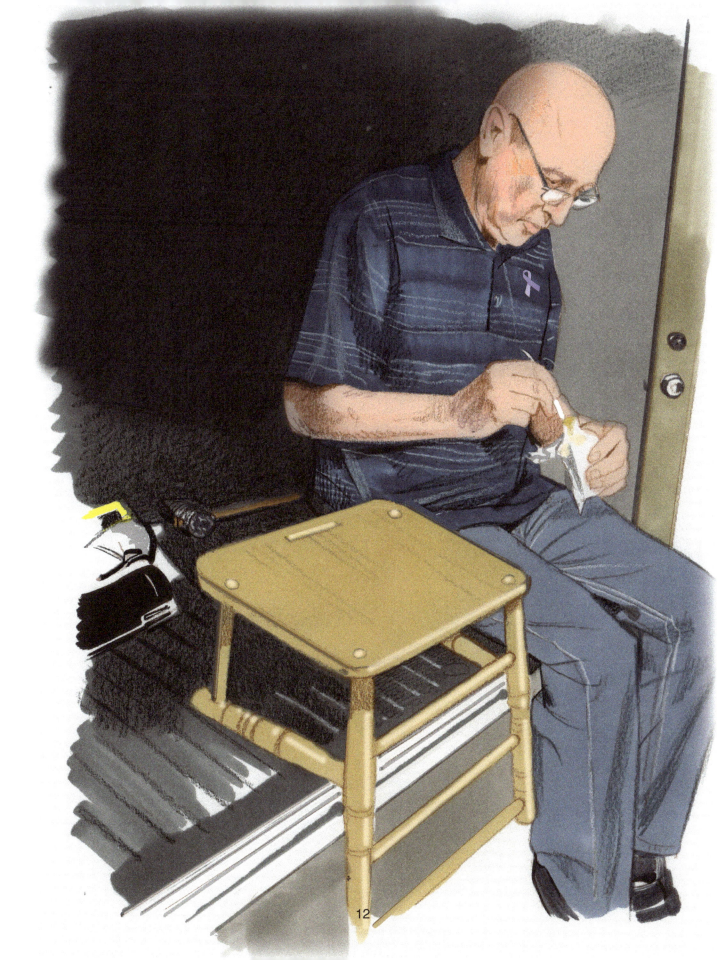

My grandma was quick to go and get her sewing kit. She took some leftover floral cloth and cut out a pattern in the shape of the new seat. She stuffed the cushion pocket with fluffy stuffing, and to it she sewed little ties so it would not slip off. Finally, the chair was ready for me.

It was not long after that that I was born. *Periwinkle has come into the world.* What a joyous day for my grandma and grandpa. They rushed to the hospital to see me. Grandpa was so proud when he first held me. He was beaming from ear to ear. No doubt, at that moment, he was imagining me rocking in that little chair.

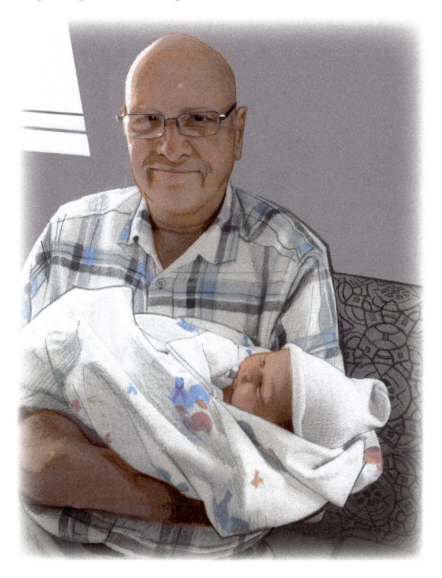

When I was born, my grandpa had been sick for a while. They say he was always positive even though he did not feel well at times. He enjoyed a happy and healthy life before this illness and was not going to let it get him down.

He always looked forward to the last snow melt and for spring to arrive. Then he could take his place in his precious garden, which had been his life's greatest joy. He tended to his garden as if each plant and flower were a baby of his own.

The secret to his garden could not be put into words. It was a love that came from within that could not be easily explained.

Summer came and went. Fall arrived, and my grandpa had to have surgery to remove the bad that was inside. He went through many months of recovery but never returned to his old self. It seemed that everyone had done their very best to help him, but it was not to be. The doctors at the hospital said it was time for him to go home, rest, and be with family and friends. He spent eight happy days with us before he passed away peacefully.

Many weeks later, when I went to visit my grandma, I saw something from across the room. It was a little chair. *Where did this chair come from?* That day it just magically appeared! I saw it, and knew it was mine.

I scrambled to it. I wondered how to get into it. Wobbly as I was, climbing into that rocking chair was not easy to do. After all, I was still learning to walk. *Plop!* Finally, I sat in my chair.

That day I climbed in and out of it a hundred times. I toppled over again and again, but did not give up.

Each time I go to my grandma's house, I look for my chair. It is always there waiting for me.

I am glad my name is Periwinkle, like the flower, because my grandpa loved his flowers. Although I will not grow up to know him, I feel such happiness in my heart. He has given me a *forever* treasure. I will always remember him with enormous joy through my chair, his story, photos of him, and his beautiful garden full of periwinkle.

Not "The End", just "The Beginning…"

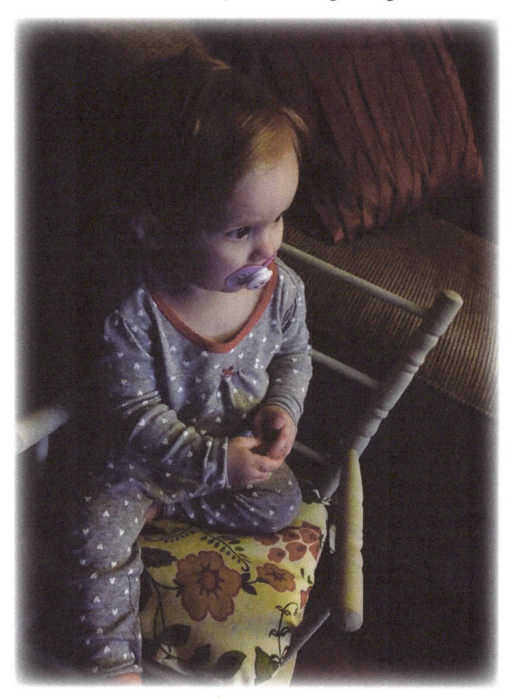

Eternal Spring

We run, we skip, we laugh and sing
For well we should! The time is spring!
   The nights are short—the days are long,
When springtime calls to summer's throng.
We run, we skip, we laugh and sing
But then a bruise, a bump on the knee,
   God reminds us of our mortality!
   Sometimes when life is at its best—
When all seems calm, at peace, at rest,
   The reality that we are dust
For God reminds us as He must!
   This life was given here on Earth,
Some years back, upon our birth,
   For all to Him, we shall return.
For deep inside, our souls we yearn,
   To go to Him for in His rest,
It's spring and summer at its best!
   To run, to skip, to laugh and sing,
To Him eternal praises bring.
We run, we skip, we laugh and sing,
Thanks be to God for Eternal Spring.

—Neil John Zeilenga
(Grandpa)
Published in Lyrical Heritage
The National Library of Poetry (1996)

A Time for Everything

³There is a time for everything,
and a season for every activity under the heavens:

²a time to be born and a time to die,
a time to plant and a time to uproot,

³a time to kill and a time to heal,
a time to tear down and a time to build,

⁴a time to weep and a time to laugh,
a time to mourn and a time to dance,

⁵a time to scatter stones and a time to gather them,
a time to embrace and a time to refrain from embracing,

⁶a time to search and a time to give up,
a time to keep and a time to throw away,

⁷a time to tear and a time to mend,
a time to be silent and a time to speak,

⁸a time to love and a time to hate,
a time for war and a time for peace.

(Ecclesiastes 3 NIV)

CPSIA information can be obtained
at www.ICGtesting.com
Printed in the USA
BVHW021738050321
601818BV00014B/1974